INTRODUCTION

Welcome to this the fourteenth book in the *"Around"* series and the return to North Somerset as this volume earlier books *Around Saltford* published in March 2003 and *Around Pensford* published in May 2006, and starts at the small village of Marksbury, and takes you on through surrounding villages to be centred on the community of Timsbury, with excursions to Peasedown St John, Camerton; Clutton and Temple Cloud. Much of the area covered by this book is based over the Somerset Coalfield, and many of the original communities grew out of the mining industry, although today all that remains are cone shaped hills disguising the old slag heaps, and miners cottages converted into commuters residencies. Life as a miner and as a miner's family was extremely harsh with few comforts, and it was not unknown for whole families to be working in the coal industry, with women and girls involved in sorting and grading coal aboveground, whilst their menfolk worked around the pithead and underground. Boys as young as six and seven spent long hours in the depth of darkness opening/closing ventilator doors, and as they became older they were used as human power to pull tubs of material from the coalface to the shaft, and to do so they wore a leather belt round their waist, from which hung a metal chain that would go between their legs to be attached to the tub enabling them to pull the tub whilst being on their hands and knees. The belt was know as a guss, and the connecting hook on the tub was known as a crook, hence the unusual name of one of the local pubs, the *Guss and Crook*. One of the villages not based upon coal is Marksbury, which sits in the shadow of Stantonbury Hill on which there are the remains of an Early Iron Age hill fort. Almost certainly Marksbury owes its existence to the rich fertile productive and relatively flat land around the base of the hill that could easily be farmed. Close to Marksbury are the villages of Priston and Farmborough, and whilst the former is also a non-mining community, the discovery and subsequent mining of coal consolidated Farmborough's community. A little further away is a village with the intriguing name of Temple Cloud, and whilst it is probable that it has some connection with the Knights Templars, there is no positive attachment, in fact the original "main" village was nearby Cameley, but during the eighteenth century the turnpike road from Bristol was constructed along the lines of the present A37, and this lead to a gradual migration of the Cameley villagers to the turnpike, and the development of Temple Cloud, which prospered whilst almost encapsulating the original village, particularly the church of St James. Such was this stagnation that during the 1950's the then Poet Laureate Sir John Betjeman, described St James as a "Rip-Van-Winkle" church, looking as though it had been asleep for a century and a half.

The preparation of this book would not have been possible without the help of those who have kindly pointed me in the right direction to identify the position of the old photographs; Ken Scotcher for his valued information, Sheila Brooks for reading and correcting the transcript and Mike Tozer for allowing me to use some of his pictures. At all times I have endeavoured to minimise any mistakes made but should any exist then they are unfortunately of my own making, for which I apologise and trust that they will not distract you from enjoying the remaining contents.

May 2009   Ian S. Bishop

The main road through Marksbury, with an open top car passing a mother and child on a warm summers day despite the smoke drifting from one of the chimneys. With the village school perched above the surrounding properties, all appears to be well in this rural enchantment, c1928.

From this angle Church Farm appears to be an extension of St Peter's and clearly shows the dominating features of the four twenty feet oversize pinnacles, each with its own weather vane. Whilst they all appear to be incongruous and are not attractive to all, there is no doubt that they have become a focal point on the very busy road that bypasses the main area of the village. c1926

With the duck pond living up to its name, Court Farm ~ Reginald and George Tibbetts ~ is reflected in the still water, c1928

Although a similar view to the previous picture the clock has moved on, more ivy has grown on the farmhouse, the pond no longer has that pristine look about it, and the ducks are not welcombed, c1935

COURT FARM, MARKSBURY.

A young lady poses on the bank of Court Farm pond as the ducks gather for the handful of feed about to be thrown in their direction Could this be the farmer's daughter? c1928

Looking down onto the central road feature and the unique arrangement of having at the road junction a retaining wall to contain the contours of the village. To the left is *Becket's Place* partially hidden by the trees planted in the grass triangle, whilst further along the road is a solitary pony and trap delivering coal, c1908

MARKSBURY SCHOOL.

The children have, together with their teacher been allowed to gather in front of the village school to satisfy the wishes of the photographer, whilst at the same time the boys in dark clothes, have been segregated from the girls all in their white dresses. Those in the front are just about tall enough to see over the hedge. Although posted in 1922, the picture was almost certainly taken at least ten years earlier.

Looking along the main street with the village school in the middle background, c1908

A close up of part of the retaining wall, as the road turns left and takes the traveller down the valley towards Court Farm, c1908

From the air we can see the full extent of Bence's Garage as it nestles in the fork created by the divergence of the A368 from the A39 as it sweeps around the bottom of the picture on its way to Hallatrow and beyond. Baled hay is being taken from the large cultivated field to the right, as a solitary estate car approaches the old style petrol pumps. Cars and Land Rovers are parked on the surrounding "waste land", whilst others are just visible tucked inside the garage workshop, c1965 *by kind permission of David Roberts*

General View, Priston.

Nº114

The camera has been moved across the cultivated fields to provide a panoramic view of Priston Hill with the ancient church of St Luke's stone built tower built, in the early decorated style, silhouetted against the skyline, c1925

The old corn mill complete with a twenty-five foot diameter overshot water wheel, c1935

A family group including a young child in a homemade handcart pause from climbing the hill to have their picture taken on a rather dull sunless day. On the left the lower hedge has been roughly trimmed, whilst on the right cottages show the ribbon development of this small village, c1931

FARMBOROUGH.

A general view over looking the old mining village of Farmborough towards the ancient parish church of All Saints with its Perpendicular tower containing a clock and six bells, c1908

A staged picture of the new owners taken by Mr Norton in 1932, and sent to the Rev. H Ketchley in Yorkshire with the following message: *"this is your old pony Polly, she is still good for six miles an hour! We call her Topsy"*

There is a great deal of information to study in this picture, of *Prospect Tea Garden*s in addition to being a Tea Garden, it is also the headquarters of the Chief Consul of Somerset, a place of accommodation for cyclists from around 4/6 [0.22$^1/_2$ p] per night, plus being a provider of Hot and Cold Luncheons. A Morris saloon HV6942 has stopped and an elderly gentleman, and perhaps his grandson pause on the steps before proceeding to sample that which is on offer, c 1936

Cottages bathe in the warmth of the summer sunshine as water in a manmade ravine trickles past the front gate of *Greentops* on the right, and *Brookside* to the left, beyond which is "Poor Hill". The card from which this picture has been taken is signed by Lily, and reads "Happy Memories of our school days, our little shop where we used to spend our pennies and halfpennies", c 1935

54314. The Ford, Farmborough, Nr. Bath.

Clouds form the backdrop of the fields that surround ivy covered *Conygre House*, which is adjacent to the Conygre Brook ford in Loves Lane; today trees shield the house, and a non-descript bridge has replaced the ford, c1958

The lone pine tree takes centre stage of the picture and it is difficult to notice a lady holding a young child who has stopped to look back at the photographer as he takes this particular view of The Street, c1910

A multiview greetings card showing the local school, New Road and the parish church of St Mary on a background of ferns and daisies, c1910

SOUTHVIEW, TIMSBURY

The Radford Hill turning can just be seen on the right, as the gentleman stands outside *"Valley View"*, c1904

Newmans Lane basking in the autumn sunshine, looking towards North Road, whilst it continues behind the camera to The Square, c1958.

Newmans Lane, Timsbury.

From the previous picture, the camera has not only been moved back along Newmans Road, but has also moved back in time. Here the photo-grapher has gathered a small group of ladies, and a dog to stand still long enough for this superb picture to be constructed. Elm cottages and The Elms form the bulk of the background, c1903

Trees dominate this scene, allowing, in their full glory, a small amount of speckled sunshine to help lighten the picture, to which the photographer has arranged for a young man and boy to stand near the camera animating what would otherwise be a rather dull picture, c1910

John Elliott's retail
beer outlet, c1908

A charming group of young Morris
Dancers ready to perform at Timsbury's
Summer Fete held on the 17th June 1909.
The third girl from the left in the back
row has been identified as Lily, whilst the
two boys at either end of the front row are
Sid and Frank respectively, perhaps
bothers and sister.

Hillside House, Timsbury, a substantial property in its own grounds, c1905

Children together with a sprinkling of adults have all come out to watch the strange antics of a man and a camera as he captures forever this moment in time at the bend in Church Lane The dominant building in this picture is now known as *Church Cottage:* the path to St Mary can be seen on the left, c1904

THE SCHOOL TIMSBURY.

The Public Elementary School for mixed junior and infant children erected in South Road during 1830, and subsequently enlarged to accommodate up to 300 pupils. Headmaster at the time of the photograph was Albert Arnold, turning on left is Mill Lane, c1912

Timsbury House is a fine old Tudor style mansion, built in 1610 and subsequently the home of the principal landowners in the area including the local Conygre coal pits, the Palmer-Samborne's, Demolished in 1961 it was reputedly haunted by a ghostly lady who wore a silk dress, and perfume, c1905

The old and overgrown canal slowly winds its way through the valley; whist trees on the right shield the lady and her dog who sit for the benefit of the photographer. According to information the lady is Miss Hodder who was a teacher, and ran a small shop in Timsbury, c1905

YUCCA PLANT IN BLOOM AT MESSRS. ROSSITERS' NURSERIES, TIMSBURY. BATH. AUG. 1909.

Looking up the 2 foot $4\frac{1}{2}$ inch gauge incline of Lower Conygre Colliery towards the pithead, winding gear and ventilation chimney, and showing a jumble of track that does not seem to be in any way conducive to the free running of the ladened trucks. With what appears to be large flat stones in the left hand trucks this is almost certainly a posed photograph, with the bowler-hatted foreman ensuring that he is included in the picture. Constructed in 1900, it was closed six years latter, c1904

A group of children, plus a guardian and her dog, and a halter held horse have been carefully positioned by the photographer towards the top of Radford Hill, with the *New Inn* and South Road overlooking the scene, c1906

A working view of Lower Conygre Pit in its twilight years, with the twin pithead wheels and chimney looking down onto screening shed a somewhat cluttered yard and the shed covering the shaft through which the loaded tram wagons were brought to the surface from a depth in excess of 1,000 feet, for the contents to be sorted and graded before being tipped into individual owners railway wagons, and then taken the six hundred yards or so the branch line at Radford & Timsbury Halt, and ultimately on to Bristol ~ note F H Silvey of Fishponds wagon in front of the picture ~ or Bath, c1908

For this view of Lower Conygre Pit the camera has crossed the yard, past the winding gear to the loading bay on the other side of the pithead, and shows the original ornamental chimneystack in all its glory. Apparently the wealthy owner of the pit could see the stack from his home at Timsbury House and had this castellated collar incorporated into the stonework so that the industrial chimney, necessary for him to make additional money, was a more pleasing feature on the skyline, perhaps in this way he could forget the dangers, dirt and hard work put in by his colliers to make all that money for him, c1903

Upper Conygre Timsbury. 69.

Possibly the owners of Upper Conygre pit stand in front of the sorting and loading shed with the single pulley wheel in the background, towards the end of the pit's viable life. Tiles are missing from part of the roof, and little working activity appears to be underway. All coal from this pit was taken away by road until 1858 when Lower Conygre Pit was opened, which allowed small coal to be sent there for onward despatch by canal, c1911

Children play in the grass watched over by two, rather stern Edwardian ladies, both sporting large flowered hats, whilst behind them Radford Hill can be seen snaking its way up towards South Road. On the extreme right is South Road Methodist Church c1905

Timsbury. 28.

In North Street a group of young men together with one young woman idle away their time outside Tabor Chapel, whilst a pony and trap wait patiently for its owner to complete his/her shopping, c1907

North Street, Timsbury.

A similar but significantly different shot of North Street to the one on the previous page is included so that the subtle variances between both pictures can be spotted, c1903

Unlike the picture reproduced on page 20, this view shows the summer foliage arching over the roadway to form a natural tunnel, with the occasional glimpses of sunlight relieving the continuing shadow, c1912

NEW RD. TIMSBURY. 2

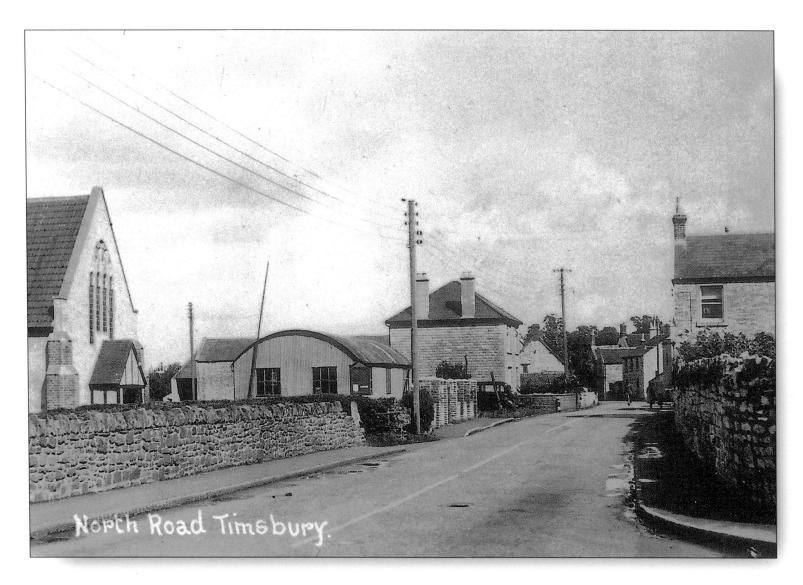

North Road just past its junction with Lyppiatt Lane, with the Congregational Church on the corner, c1936

Possibly at the behest of the man with a camera the cyclist stops and poses as he adroitly leans over his machine in the typical casual mode of one so used to having his picture taken, on the other hand of course he could just be nosy and wondering what is going on; in any case he was determined to get his picture taken. Whatever the truth we have here a row of fine houses overlooking South View, and stretching from the corner of Maggs Hill to the properties adjacent to the Methodist Church, c1929

The photographer has carefully collected a mixed group of villagers in South Road ranging from a young girl with a large flowered hat, to young lads wearing a mixture of clothes, to miners on their way home. All stand in a self-conscious pose, totally unused to the antics of a man who keeps disappearing under a black cloak, and who instructs them all to stand still. How many among the villagers present will have realised that they are partaking in a moment of history that has been frozen in time for generations to come to see and appreciate. The *New Inn* built 1703 ~ now known as the *Guss and Crook* ~ is to the right next to Church Hill, whilst three women watch the proceedings from afar in Church Lane c1908.

Part way along Lansdown View with the gate of number 10, and numbers 11 and 12 on the left, whilst to the right of the latter property is the gap subsequently in filled by 12A and 13A. Further along the road, some of the residents have come out to see what is happening at a time when the camera was still a novelty only available to the wealthy, c1910

At this point Newmans Lane has reached The Square, with *Apley House* on the right, and a horse and cart about to descend Maggs Hill, whilst in the centre of the picture, the photographer has carefully crafted a row of young girls all in their smart white pinafore dresses outside the local drapers/grocers. Note the clock and the sign for Cadbury's chocolates, c1904

For this picture the position of the camera has been moved further into The Square, and slightly turned to the left to capture more of the sun faced buildings, and the entrance of Maggs Hill and sight of Oakhill House and the Christadelphian Chapel, and the start of Rectory Lane behind the boy with the baskets. To the right is the village Post Office and stationers with Mrs Ida Cox in charge, c1912

HIGH ST TIMSBURY. 21.

From the corner of Maggs Hill with The Square, the camera is now pointing down the High Street, with the draper/grocers shop on the left alongside Sid Sims front room hairdressing salon, an unidentified shop believed to be the general store known as Bart's Bazaar, and the old police station. On the opposite side of the street is Walton House, c1906

With the lady's dogs being closely watched by another canine across the road, The Square has an air of tranquillity and wealth, with left to right, Apsley House; Elm Cottages, and The Elms all soaking up the summer sunshine, c1905

In contrast to the previous picture, the camera has been moved back to the apex of Maggs Hill, and brought the further images closer to the lens, and instead of a relatively empty square, the photographer has filled the space with most of the village children, placing both boys and girls across most of its width. Many of the children would probably have not fully understood that their images were about to be frozen in time, and few would have had the opportunity of seeing their image when the picture was published, c1910

A small passenger train approaches Radford and Timsbury Halt, to collect the few travellers and take them onto Hallatrow and beyond. This was one of the few stations that could boast a brick built station building and gas lighting. Behind the photographer there existed a passing loop, and a 600 yard siding that served Lower Conygre Colliery c1906

A set of different vignette views makes up this c1912 greetings card of Peasedown St John, and includes external and internal views of St John built in the early 1890's, Dunkerton colliery, which in its short working life of around twenty-years became the largest pit in the Somerset Coalfield, plus Bath Road, and Lower Peasedown.

Looking down Bath Road from its junction with Belle View Close, the cottage on the extreme right is *Mont Rose,* c1906

A group of children have been positioned by the photographer in a small un-named road just off Bath Road, in this panoramic view looking over the newly constructed Hillside View, c1908

The push and pull train waits to have its photograph taken with a group of men standing on the platform, but sadly the number of railway officials appear to outnumber the potential customers. The length of the platform seems excessive to the size of the train, and behind the station buildings the winding gear and chimney of the Camerton Old pit can be seen, whilst in front of the train is the Camerton Hill Road Bridge, c 1906

CAMERTON STATION. 14.

Although this appears to be a busy moment in this little station's working day, careful study will show that the train has been held up to allow the photographer to climb up to the over road bridge to capture a different view on the same day. Here we can see the extent of the sidings and the controlling brick built signal box, but out of view the track divides with the left hand 1882 built branch line running to New Pit Colliery, whilst the right-hand track continues on its way to Limpley Stoke, c1906

New Pit Offices not long after they had been constructed. Under this stretch of road flows the Somerset Coal Canal, with both stonewalls forming the parapets of the bridge, c1905

The surface working area of New Pit, with pithead gear clearly visible, as is a group of coal tubs ready to be taken to the screening shed, c1905

46

The Upper Bristol Road sweeps up the hill from Temple Cloud as it passes the entrance to the Rectory. Further up the hill on the left is the Hinton Blewett turning and the old brewery, whilst on the right is the "Old Bake House" with Frederick Blacker stone and marble mason business that was first established in the eighteenth century, c1910

The much restored church of St Augustine, including the twelfth-century chancel arch and doorway. The dominant reddish sandstone tower dates from the seventeen hundreds, 1910

A270.   Clutton.

It is possible that it is the photographer who has lent his motorcycle against the wall in order that he can take this view along a very quiet Station Road, with both the Methodist Chapel and the Independents Chapel seen on the left, whilst on the right a young lad with a parcel under his arm comes out of Church Lane, c1930

Post Office, Glutton.

7961

An early motorcycle combination stands outside the entrance to the village Post Office, whilst an elderly villager stands by to see what is the commotion that is upsetting the tranquillity of Station Road. The picture has been taken from a Happy Birthday Greetings Card posted on the 2nd June 1923

The camera has been moved around to be nearly face on with the building, as we are taken back almost twenty years from the date of the previous picture and given a further opportunity of looking back at a specific moment in time. The vehicular use of the combustion engine is a few years away, and the horse is still the main power source of wheeled motion on the roads. With two young boys standing either side of a poorly displayed shop window there is an air if not of neglect but of poverty in this c1904 picture.

The entrance to Clutton railway station opened on the 3rd September 1873 and closed in the mid 1960's. The signal box can be seen above the group of small children, and to the right of the cottages the top of the station buildings and the platform canopy is visible, c1910

This picture taken from inside the station provides us with a much better view of the brick built Signal Box, the adjacent extensive goods sidings, and the large ornate canopy. How useful such a station would be today, c1959

A lone passenger having missed the last train by a year or so exits the station, which seems devoid of all railway activity and is shortly to fall asleep, never again to be awakened. Closed to passengers on the 2nd November 1959, this so useful country station was entirely closed on the 10th June 1963. Picture c1961

The junction of Station Road with Upper Bristol Road with a group of cloth capped workmen having come out of their engineering place of work, together with the foreman to have their picture taken, although all of them seem somewhat self-conscious in the variety of poses taken. With a large cup and saucer hanging in the doorway of the larger property, there is a similar sign on the steps both with the notation Nectar Tea, subsequently this building was occupied by Rogers suppliers of animal feedstuffs, c1912

The Rectory, later *Cholwell Hall* looks majestically over the surrounding grounds, as the A37 hurries around the boundary before following the tree line up the hill to Clutton. On the left an early motor vehicle with the registration mark Y322 appears to have broken down, whilst the driver of the dog cart looks back in the knowledge that for the time being his horse is more reliable than that new fangled machine, c1910

The camera has been brought to the hub of the village, and the author of the postcard has kindly identified the orientation of the picture. *Temple Inn* can be seen on the left, with the Police Court taking centre stage, c1903

With substantial tree foliage dominating the picture, we are at the junction of the main Upper Bristol Road (A37) with Cameley Road on the left. Hidden behind the right-hand foliage is *Walcott Cottage* and just beyond is the start of Gillets Hill Lane, c1922

For this picture the camera has been positioned in Eastcourt Road to clearly show the junction with the A37 as it looks back towards "Old Stores Cottage". Near to the parked cycle is the entrance to the local Pandora's Box of sweets and childhood goodies, and was forever known by the children of the village as the "sweetie shop", whilst above the shop you could have your hair cut, c1937

The main village stores advertising Fry's Cocoa, and Hovis Bread and biscuits. The news that a man with a camera was taking pictures soon circulated the village, and by the time that the camera equipment had been set up, a number of the local children with one or two adults have turned up to see what is going on, c1912.

Looking down Perrin Close to J Appleby & Sons village store in Cameley Road, whilst the staff stand in the doorway to welcome, perhaps the first customer of the day, who has arrived in a small pony and trap, c1904

The existence of the General Store in Cameley Lane has by now been totally obliterated, but the adjoining *Matson House* still exists: perhaps it is the Appleby sons who stand in the doorway of the shop in this c1910 picture.

The Refuge in the guise of a castle turret, looks down on the triangular shaped green, formed by the double junction of Cameley Road and the Upper Bristol A37 road, with its Somersetshire County Council directional finger post clearly visible, whilst to the left of the "castle" is *Walcott Cottage* c1912

59

Main Road, Temple Cloud.

Unlike the previous picture the bright sunshine in this illustration picks out all of the different architectural features of this group of properties as we look up the hill towards the judicial hub of the village, and the introduction of the first phase of the internal combustion engine in the form of motor vehicles, how things will change in the future, c1934

Main Road, Temple Cloud.

A lady pushes her bike up the hill having just passed or just been in William Chivers emporium, purveyor of top quality fresh meat, whilst on the opposite side of the road another cyclist needs to shield his eyes from the glare of the sun as he speeds his way down the hill. Further up the hill a group of cloth capped men are shown the novelty of one of those new fangled machines, which are now coming to the village in ever increasing numbers, in fact there is even another one on the brow of the hill, c1934

The gates mark the entrance to *Oxford House*, whilst the cottage on the corner of Cameley Road and Cameley Close is aptly called *Little Corner*. Note the young man hanging over his bicycle absorbed with curiosity at what is going on, c1912

The driver of the farm cart looks back over his shoulder not sure as to what is happening behind him on this quite peaceful day. On the left is *Temple Inn* waiting for its rush of customers that hopefully will occur later in the day, c1910

Two pairs of semi-detached houses have been built high above the main road with access through Gillets Hill Lane just visible on the right. Taken from a card written from *Long Close* and posted on the 8th August 1933

Main Road, Temple Cloud.

Main Road, Temple Cloud.

The Upper Bristol Road (A37) is shown as a quiet country lane sweeping down the hill on its way to the Mendips. Two men idly exchange the state of the World, whilst a small car is almost lost from view in the background of the foliage. On the left the vicarage stands in apparent isolation, c1935

Stanley House stands at the junction of the A37 with Cameley Road, with the outbuilding on the right now Cameley Surgery. Further down the hill behind the electric pole is the building now known as *Old Stores Cottage* recalling the earlier use of that property, c1935.